LET

Hunting
QUAIL and
PHEASANTS

Hines Lambert

PowerKiDS press.

New York

Published in 2013 by The Rosen Publishing Group, Inc.
29 East 21st Street, New York, NY 10010

First Edition

Editor: Amelie von Zumbusch
Book Design: Kate Laczynski

Photo Credits: Background graphic © iStockphoto.com/Andrea Zanchi; sidebar binoculars © iStockphoto.com/Feng Yu; cover John Cancalosi/Peter Arnold/Getty Images; p 4 Brett Billings/USFWS; pp. 5, 7, 27 iStockphoto/Thinkstock; p. 6 Tony Campbell/Shutterstock.com; p. 9 Robynrg/Shutterstock.com; pp. 10, 13, 15 Wichita Eagle/McClatchy-Tribune/Getty Images; p. 11 John and Karen Hollingsworth/USFWS; pp. 12, 15, 19 Kansas City Star/McClatchy-Tribune/Getty Images; p. 16 Shaun Heasley/Stringer/Getty Images; p. 17 Sacramento Bee/McClatchy-Tribune/Getty Images; pp. 18, 21 (right) Linn Currie/Shutterstock.com; p. 20 Iurii Konoval/Shutterstock.com; p. 21 (left) artur gabrysiak/Shutterstock.com; p. 22 Miami Herald/McClatchy-Tribune/Getty Images; p. 23 Steve & Dave Maslowski/Photo Researchers/Getty Images; p. 24 © iStockphoto.com/kali9; p. 25 Maxim Lysenko/Shutterstock.com; p. 26 (left) Brian Kennedy/Workbook Stock/Getty Images; p. 26 (right) Alexandra Grablewski/The Image Bank/Getty Images; p. 28 Gallo Images/Danita Delimont/the Agency Collection/Getty Images; p. 29 © iStockphoto.com/DIGIcal.
Interactive eBook Only: p. 5 Wichita Eagle/McClatchy-Tribune/Getty Images; pp. 7, 26 iStockphoto/Thinkstock; p. 7 Tony Campbell/Shutterstock.com; p. 7 Wild Horizon/Universal Images Group/Getty Images; p. 7 USFWS; p. 7 Roberta Olenick/All Canada Photos/Getty Images; p. 9 Simon Krzic/iStockfootage/Getty Images; p. 11 Herbert Kratky/Shutterstock.com; p. 13 © iStockphoto.com/Andrew Hyslop; p. 15 DOTV/Shutterstock.com; p. 16 © iStockphoto.com/Jason Doiy; p. 19 Joel Sartore/National Geographic/Getty Images; p. 22 J Breedlove/Shutterstock.com; p. 24 Bobby Deal/RealDealPhoto/Shutterstock.com; p. 28 Jorge Viamonte/iStockfootage/Getty Images.

Library of Congress Cataloging-in-Publication Data

Lambert, Hines.
 Hunting quail and pheasants / by Hines Lambert. — 1st ed.
     p. cm. — (Let's go hunting)
 Includes index.
 ISBN 978-1-4488-9664-6 (library binding) — ISBN 978-1-4488-9786-5 (pbk.) —
 ISBN 978-1-4488-9787-2 (6-pack)
 1. Quail shooting—Juvenile literature. 2. Pheasant shooting—Juvenile literature. I. Title.
 SK325.Q2L36 2013
 799.2'4627—dc23
                                    2012028253

Manufactured in the United States of America

CPSIA Compliance Information: Batch #W13PK2: For Further Information contact Rosen Publishing, New York, New York at 1-800-237-9932

CONTENTS

Upland Game Hunting

Upland game birds, such as pheasants and quail, provide some of the most exciting hunting in the United States. Upland game birds are wild birds that are not found on the water. They include quail, pheasants, grouse, and several others. Not only do these birds taste great, they are fun to hunt. Most upland game hunters bring their dogs along on their hunts.

Many hunters enjoy upland game hunting with their families.

Some male quail, such as this California quail, have curled head feathers called plumes.

Quail and pheasant hunts provide an excellent chance to enjoy being outdoors with your family. Many hunters enjoy shooting at flying birds, or **wing shooting**. Most states allow large **bag limits** on upland game birds. A bag limit is how many birds a hunter may kill. This means that unlike many hunters, upland game hunters may take several birds during a hunt.

Quail

Gambel's quail are named after the American scientist William Gambel. Gambel lived in the first half of the nineteenth century.

The quail is a small game bird that lives all over the world. There are 130 **species** of quail, and 6 are **native** to the United States or Canada. Quail can be found in 44 of the 50 US states. However, the northern bobwhite is the only species of quail found east of the Mississippi River. Unfortunately, some species, such as the northern bobwhite, have low **populations**.

Quail prefer to live in thick brush that is close to open fields. Their feathers are usually brown, tan, or white and have interesting patterns. These colors and patterns help quail **camouflage** themselves in their surroundings. Most quail eat berries and seeds. They also feed on roots, leaves, and insects. A group of quail is called a covey. A covey can have fewer than 10 quail or as many as 100!

Did You Know?

California quail enjoy taking dust baths together. They roll in the dust and flap their wings to raise dust clouds.

Northern bobwhites get their name because their call sounds like "bob-white" or "bob-bob-white."

7

Pheasants

Pheasants are also game birds, but they are much larger than quail. There are about 50 species of pheasants in the world. Male pheasants, or cocks, often have brightly colored feathers. Females, or hens, often have dull colors. This coloring allows hens to blend in with their surroundings. Cocks protect hens by attracting predators with their bright colors.

Like quail, pheasants split their time between open fields and brush. Male pheasants usually gather a group of female pheasants to mate with. Sometimes male pheasants fight over the females. These are often fights to the death! Males have spurs on their legs that they use as weapons. The ring-necked pheasant is one of the most common birds in North America, but it is actually native to Asia.

Ring-necked pheasants are also called common pheasants. They can measure up to 34 inches (86 cm) from wingtip to wingtip.

Did You Know?

Pheasants swallow small stones, gravel, or tough seeds. These objects stay in the birds' gizzards, or stomachs, to help break food down into small pieces.

Each state has different hunting laws for upland game birds. Visit your state's website to learn these. Some states, such as Missouri, have special upland hunting seasons for young hunters. In youth seasons, adults are allowed to hunt with young hunters, but they are not allowed to shoot. This is a perfect chance to practice wing shooting.

Bag limits are in place to make sure that animals are not overhunted.

Someone who works for the US Fish and Wildlife Service, or FWS, might also be able to answer some of your questions about hunting laws.

Each state sets a different bag limit on upland game birds. Pheasant bag limits are often lower than quail bag limits. This makes sense because pheasants provide more meat than quail. Some states allow quail bag limits of 10 or more. Bag limits help bird populations stay healthy. They are very important for the future of these birds. Pheasants were overhunted in the past, and some quail populations have been low in recent years.

Good Boots and Lots of Orange

Think about quail and pheasant **habitat** when you plan your hunt. Since these birds often hide in dense brush, it is a good idea to wear thick pants that can protect you from rips and cuts. Upland game hunters usually walk long distances during a hunt. Make sure you have good boots that are well broken in. Sore feet can spoil a good hunt!

It is a smart idea to have your hunting dog wear the same bright orange color that hunters do.

Quail and pheasant hunts often take place in chilly weather. Remember to dress warmly for your hunt!

Your state's hunting laws will probably require that you wear bright orange. This color helps other hunters see you. Most hunters wear orange hats along with orange vests or coats.

Remember to bring tools to **field dress** your kills. Carry a sharp hunting knife and scissors. Some coats and vests have big pockets for carrying your kills. A game bag to carry your kills is also a good option.

When and Where

Before you hunt, learn how quail and pheasants spend their days. Quail usually go to an open field to eat early in the morning. They find cover in brush during the middle of the day and return to a field to feed in the early evening.

Pheasants follow a similar daily pattern. These birds rarely travel far. Cold weather may cause them to stay in cover all day. Pheasants are often found along streams, in ditches, and along fences. Some hunters drive around before a hunt and look for pheasants from their cars.

If you want to hunt on private land, remember to ask the owner first. Sometimes hunters must pay to hunt on private land. Your state might own public land where hunting is allowed. Check online for more information.

This upland game hunter is hunting quail in Kansas. Both scaled quail and northern bobwhites are found in Kansas.

Flushing

When hunting with a group, spread out and walk in a straight horizontal line. This way no one will end up in the line of fire.

You can only shoot at birds you can see. Quail and pheasants are good at hiding. The trick is to find their hiding spots and startle them into the open. This is called **flushing** them. Some hunters use quail calls. Quail call to each other when they are startled. A good quail call can fool an entire covey into thinking a hunter is a quail.

Two or more hunters can cover a lot more ground than just one hunter. They can also work together to flush birds. A pheasant hunter can wait at the top of a hill while another hunter walks through brush at the bottom of the hill. Since pheasants run uphill, any birds flushed will run toward the first hunter.

Upland hunters should walk into the wind. This lets dogs get strong scents. It also keeps the birds from hearing or smelling the hunters coming.

Bird Dogs

Dogs are far better hunters than humans. Some kinds of dogs were actually bred for upland hunting. They know how to find birds, how to flush them, and often how to retrieve them for their masters. Some upland hunting dogs are trained to run through brush in a zigzag pattern. This confuses and startles the birds. They might jump out of cover or try to fly away. A hunter in the right position might have an easy wing shot.

Bring water for your dog! Dogs tend to get thirsty on a long day of hunting and that can be unhealthy for them.

Dogs that are trained to hunt and retrieve birds are known as bird dogs. This bird dog just retrieved a quail for the hunters who shot it.

Other dogs can show hunters the location of birds by moving their heads and positioning their bodies. Some of these dogs even point to birds by holding very still. Many dogs will wait for their masters' command to find and retrieve fallen birds.

Did You Know?

Hunting dogs must be trained not to be afraid of gunshots. They must not run off or chase animals. Special trainers and camps can teach dogs to become great hunters.

Pointing, Flushing, and Retrieving

Most dogs that hunt quail and pheasants have been trained to point or flush. When a pointing dog locates a bird, it freezes. Its nose points at the bird. Good pointing dogs are trained to stay frozen while the hunter shoots. Some of the most popular pointing dogs are English setters, Irish setters, and English pointers. They are great dogs to bring on a quail hunt.

Cocker spaniels are good at both flushing and retrieving birds.

Top: *Irish setters are also known as red setters because of their reddish coats.* Right: *As you might guess from their name, German shorthaired pointers were bred for pointing.*

Flushing dogs startle birds out of tight areas so hunters can shoot. They are especially good at pheasant hunting. Spaniels are excellent flushing dogs. Some hunters use retrievers, such as Labrador retrievers and Chesapeake Bay retrievers, to flush. These dogs are bred for hunting ducks and geese, but they can be trained to flush. They are also good at finding and retrieving fallen birds.

Shotguns

These hunters are using their shotguns for a pheasant hunt in Okeechobee, Florida.

Quail and pheasant hunters use shotguns. These firearms shoot tiny pellets called shot over a small area. Since shotguns are made for small and fast-moving targets, they are perfect for wing shooting. Shotguns do not shoot very far, but pheasants and quail are small targets. They can rarely be shot farther than 20 or 30 yards (18–27 m) away.

It is important to select the correct shotgun gauge. This number is the width of the barrel. Some shotguns, such as a .10 gauge, are too powerful for small birds like quail. Gauges of .12 and .20 will work for these birds. Since you will be walking a lot, pick a shotgun that is not too heavy. Your shotgun should weigh only about 6 or 7 pounds (3 kg).

Did You Know?

Make sure your shotgun's barrel is not too long. Remember, you will need to point and shoot quickly to make wing shots.

If you have any questions about your shotgun, ask an experienced hunter.

Shooting

When wing shooting, try to aim in front of the bird in the direction it is flying. This way the bird will fly into your shot. Remember, your shotgun is a dangerous weapon and not a toy. If it can kill birds, it can also kill people and dogs. Always keep your shotgun's **safety** on until you are ready to fire. Avoid shooting at low-flying birds. You might hit a dog or another hunter.

Keep your shotgun pointed away from your dogs and other hunters at all times.

Shooting clay pigeons is popular both as practice for hunting and as a sport in its own right.

Practice will help your wing shooting. Shooting **clay pigeons** is a very fun way to practice.

Shotgun shells with lead shot can be bad for the environment. Some states do not allow hunters to use these shells for upland game hunting. Check to make sure your shotgun shells are safe before you shoot them in quail or pheasant habitat.

Food and Feathers

Quail and pheasants are delicious. In some countries, pheasants are often served on Christmas. To eat these birds safely, you must first dress and **pluck** them correctly. Be sure to research before you go hunting. Ask an adult hunter to help you cut open the birds and remove their **organs**. You should get your

Bottom: *Some pheasant hunters like to have their kills stuffed and display them in their homes.*
Right: *These quail were roasted. Quail is often cooked in the same ways chicken is.*

Some people hang their birds after they have field dressed them.

birds cold as soon as possible so that **bacteria** do not spread. Putting them in plastic bags before putting them on ice will also keep bacteria from spreading. Never eat birds that stink, have green liquid coming out of them, or have black blood. They are sick, and eating them will make you sick, too.

Hunters often keep pheasant feathers because they are so long and beautiful. They also serve as reminders of a great hunt.

Save the Birds

These California quail are at Malheur National Wildlife Refuge, in Princeton, Oregon. Wildlife refuges are areas set aside for plants and animals.

Many hunters who enjoy shooting quail and pheasant know that they must take part in protecting these birds and their habitats. Some belong to organizations like Quail Unlimited and Pheasants Forever. These groups make sure that bird populations and habitat are protected. Quail Unlimited has raised over $7 million to improve and restore quail habitats.

Pheasants Forever protects land for pheasant habitat. It has set aside more than 135,000 acres (54,633 ha) for these birds.

Young people can get involved with these organizations. They might plant trees or grow food for quail and pheasants. You can make a difference simply by picking up litter in these birds' habitats. If you enjoy hunting quail and pheasants, do your part so that someday your children can enjoy hunting them, too.

Pheasants Forever was formed in 1982. It now has more than 600 chapters, or local groups, in the United States and Canada.

HUNTING TIPS

1 Many hunters like to go pheasant hunting at the beginning of the season, when the birds are less familiar with hunters. As the season goes on, the birds get smarter.

2 Never point your shotgun at anything unless you are about to shoot at it. Keep the gun's safety on until right before you are ready to fire.

3 Before hunting season starts, scout out some good hunting spots. See where the pheasants and quail are nesting and eating.

4 Wet weather may make it easier for your dog. Moisture makes scents smell stronger.

5 Always aim for a specific quail, not a whole covey. This way, you will kill and not just injure a bird.

6 Pheasants often gather near ditches. They look for cover in the tall grasses there.

7 The first snow often confuses pheasants. During it, they can be seen out in the open or along the roads.

8 When you are dressing your bird, look in the stomach for the food it has most recently eaten. That will give you a clue of where to start hunting next time.

GLOSSARY

bacteria (bak-TIR-ee-uh) Tiny living things that cannot be seen with the eye alone. Some bacteria cause illness or rotting, but others are helpful.

bag limits (BAG LIH-muts) How many of certain kinds of animals hunters are allowed to kill.

camouflage (KA-muh-flahj) To hide by using a color and a pattern that matches one's surroundings.

clay pigeons (KLAY PIH-junz) Disks that people fire at to practice their shooting.

field dress (FEELD DRES) To remove the parts from a kill that would make the meat go bad.

flushing (FLUSH-ing) Driving something out from its hiding place.

habitat (HA-buh-tat) The kind of land where an animal or plant naturally lives.

native (NAY-tiv) Born or grown in a certain place or country.

organs (AWR-gunz) Parts inside a body that do jobs.

pluck (PLUK) To pull the feathers out of something.

populations (pop-yoo-LAY-shunz) Groups of animals or people living in the same place.

safety (SAYF-tee) A part on a gun that keeps it from being fired by mistake.

species (SPEE-sheez) One kind of living thing. All people are one species.

wing shooting (WING SHOOT-ing) The sport of shooting flying birds.

INDEX

WEBSITES

Due to the changing nature of Internet links, PowerKids
Press has developed an online list of websites related to the
subject of this book. This site is updated regularly. Please
use this link to access the list:
www.powerkidslinks.com/lgh/quail/

TITLES IN THIS SERIES

Hunting Deer

Hunting Ducks

Hunting Moose and Elk

Hunting Quail and Pheasants

Hunting Rabbits

Hunting Turkeys

PowerKiDS press

ISBN 978-1-4488-9786-5

9 781448 897865

CYF

6-PACK ISBN 978-1-4488-9787-2